Bess Wallace Truman

Bess Wallace Truman

✦✦✦✦✦✦✦✦✦✦✦✦✦✦✦✦✦✦✦✦✦✦

1885–1982

BY BARBARA SILBERDICK FEINBERG

CHILDREN'S PRESS®
A Division of Grolier Publishing
New York   London   Hong Kong   Sydney
Danbury, Connecticut

Consultants: ROBERT H. FERRELL, PH.D.
                 Author of ten books on Harry Truman, including
                 Harry S. Truman: A Life, published in 1996
                 LINDA CORNWELL
                 Learning Resource Consultant
                 Indiana Department of Education

Project Editor: DOWNING PUBLISHING SERVICES
Page Layout: CAROLE DESNOES
Photo Researcher: JAN IZZO

Visit Children's Press on the Internet at:
http://publishing.grolier.com

Library of Congress Cataloging-in-Publication Data
Feinberg, Barbara Silberdick
    Bess Wallace Truman / by Barbara Silberdick Feinberg
       p. cm. — (Encyclopedia of first ladies)
    Includes bibliographical references and index.
    Summary: Presents a biography of the wife of the thirty-third president of the
United States, a woman who preferred the privacy of family life to the public role
of First Lady.
    ISBN 0-516-21000-9
    1. Truman, Bess Wallace, 1885–1982—Juvenile literature. 2. Presidents'
spouses—United States—Biography—Juvenile literature. [1. Truman, Bess
Wallace, 1885–1982. 2. First ladies.] I. Title II. Series.
E814.1.T69   1998
973.918'092—dc21   98–7894
[B]   CIP
                                                         AC

1 2 3 4 5 6 7 8 9 10 R 07 06 05 04 03 02 01 00 99 98

Table of Contents

Bess Wallace Truman

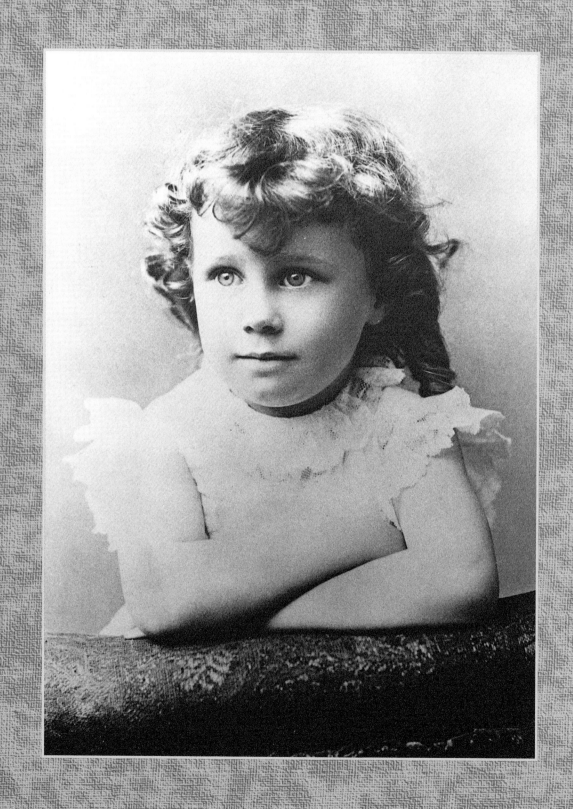

CHAPTER ONE

Growing Up in A Small Town

☆ ☆ ☆ ☆ ☆ ☆ ☆ ☆ ☆ ☆ ☆ ☆ ☆ ☆ ☆ ☆

Elizabeth Virginia Wallace, known first as Bessie and then as Bess, described her childhood as "blissful." She was born on February 13, 1885, in Independence, Missouri, about 10 miles (16 kilometers) from the center of Kansas City. It was a comfortable place to grow up. With only 6,000 residents, neighbors called one another by name and helped one another when difficulties arose. They trusted one another; after all, many families had lived in the area for generations. Blacks, however, were isolated in their own part of town and attended their own school. These former slaves and their children were not welcome to shop in

☆ ☆ ☆ ☆ ☆ ☆ ☆ ☆ ☆ ☆ ☆ ☆ ☆ ☆ ☆ ☆

Portrait of America, 1885: America Bustles

✦ ✦

What a busy place the United States was in the year Elizabeth Wallace was born! Miners, farmers, loggers, and ranchers overran the once-wild West. Nearly 100,000 miles (160,930 km) of railroads connected the Atlantic and Pacific Oceans. Telegraph wires buzzed with messages. Most modern homes had a telephone. People, ideas, and products traveled farther and faster than ever before.

Thirty-eight states and 60 million people made up the Union, and Grover Cleveland was the twenty-second president. Factories forged farm machinery, fired steel, and packed meat. Mines yielded coal and iron. Oil fields spewed crude. Many Americans grew prosperous. They built ornate homes filled with elaborate furniture. Proper ladies dressed in elegant silks and satins. The bustle—a pad or frame worn at the back of a woman's skirt and covered with material—adorned many a fashionable dress.

Author Mark Twain called this lavish period the Gilded Age. But Twain may be better remembered for his book *The Adventures of Huckleberry Finn,* published in 1885. This story about a young boy's adventures along the Mississippi River describes another America. In this age of prosperity, most Americans lived lives of work, not wealth. The number of working women nearly doubled during the 1880s. Immigrants flooded in from Europe hoping to find jobs. Many of them lived poorly in the cities. Out West, the once mighty Native American nations crowded reservations, unable to hunt or farm. Chinese immigrants, who had come to build the railroads and work the mines, faced terrible discrimination.

Nothing, however, could dampen American optimism in 1885. Two other events of that year captured perfectly the nation's soaring spirits. The first skyscraper was completed in Chicago. No big deal by today's standards at only nine stories, its revolutionary construction led to taller and taller structures. In the nation's capital, the Washington Monument, completed after 37 years, towered 555 feet (169 meters) to become the world's tallest stone monument.

Lexington Street, Independence Square, in 1909

the stores or to borrow books from the library.

Bess's parents, David Willock Wallace and Margaret "Madge" Gates Wallace were respected members of the community. David was the son of Independence mayor Benjamin Wallace. Through his father's connections, David was appointed deputy recorder of marriage licenses, a local government clerk. From 1889 to 1893, he was the treasurer of Jackson County. He later became deputy U.S. surveyor of customs for the port of Kansas City, supervising the collection of fees charged for goods brought in from foreign nations for sale in the United States. Madge was the daughter of George Porterfield Gates, who

Bess's parents were David Willock Wallace (above right) and Madge Gates Wallace (right).

11

Bess's grandfather, George Porterfield Gates

had made a small fortune manufacturing "Queen of the Pantry" flour, sold throughout the Midwest. She was accustomed to living in style as the daughter of a wealthy man. The Wallaces were married on June 13, 1883. In addition to Bess, they had three surviving children: Frank Gates Wallace, born in 1887; George Porterfield

Missouri, U.S.A.

✶ ✶

Nineteenth-century Missouri earned the nickname "Gateway to the West" because of its location on rivers and trails. To Native Americans in those parts, the name *Missouri* meant "town of the large canoes." The word reflects the importance of the Missouri River in the land's history. Part of a great network of rivers that connects the midland with the Far West, the Great Lakes, and the East Coast, the Missouri forms the western border of the state until it bends eastward. At the great bend, Kansas City (first called Westport Landing) and Independence grew to be trading posts, and later "outfitting centers" where pioneers loaded up their wagons to journey west. Two major overland trails originated in Independence. The Santa Fe Trail opened in 1821 for settlers heading to the Southwest. By the 1830s, the Oregon Trail was the best route for Northwest-bound pioneers. From St. Joseph, some 60 miles (97 km) up the Missouri, the famous Pony Express began delivery of mail to California in 1860. By Bess Wallace's day, commerce and shipping thrived along the river, and railroads had replaced the foot trails. Even Bess's father, in his post as deputy U.S. surveyor of customs for the port of Kansas City, made a living from the great Missouri River.

Wallace, born in 1892; and David Frederick Wallace, born in 1900. Another daughter died in infancy.

Bess said of her childhood, "For forgetting my manners or other misdemeanors, I was punished, but never physically and never in anger. . . . There was never much praise for things well done—that was expected

Left to right: Bess, George, and Frank Wallace

Against All Odds

★ ☆ ★ ☆ ★ ☆ ★ ☆ ★ ☆ ★ ☆ ★ ☆ ★ ☆ ★ ☆ ★ ☆ ★ ☆ ★ ☆ ★

Even though black slaves had won their freedom after the Civil War, the road to equality in the years that followed was not easy. African-Americans actually faced *decreasing* civil rights. "Jim Crow" laws made segregation and discrimination against blacks legal. Named for a comic black stage character played by a white actor, these laws kept blacks from voting. They forbade them from entering white establishments. A general mood of racism backed the laws up with lynchings and mob violence. Against these odds, Booker T. Washington started the Tuskegee Institute, the nation's leading African-American agricultural and industrial college, in 1881. Soprano Sissieretta Jones sang at the White House and toured Europe. In 1895, W. E. B. Du Bois became the first African-American to receive a Ph.D. from Harvard. Black farmers formed the Colored Farmers' Alliance to improve the lives of a million members. The U. S. 10th Colored Cavalry charged San Juan Hill with Teddy Roosevelt in the Spanish-American War. In 1909, the National Association for the Advancement of Colored People (NAACP) took root. That same year, Matthew H. Henson braved the North Pole with Commodore Robert E. Peary, sharing equally the hardships of Arctic exploration.

of me." She was very attached to her father, a charming, friendly man. On Sundays, he would take his family to the ice cream shop for a treat. Bess recalled, "He'd suggest wonderful things to do. He even made the games we played exciting adventures." A popular game was Run Sheep Run, a form of hide-and-seek.

Six-year-old Harry Truman first met five-year-old Bess in Sunday school at the Presbyterian church. He later described her as a "little blue-eyed golden-haired girl," and "the most beautiful and the sweetest person on earth." He was happiest when he could carry her books home from school. Bess, however, spent little time with the near-sighted, scrawny farmer's son. She was a tomboy, interested in a variety of sports. She was an outstanding tennis player, who also rode horseback and played baseball. With his breakable glasses, Harry couldn't participate in these activities. To help Bess become more ladylike,

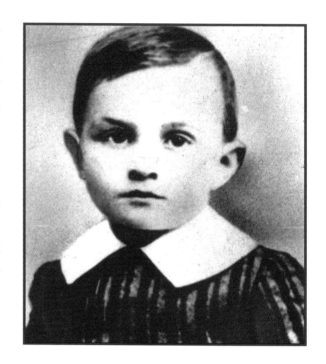

Top: Harry Truman at age four
Bottom: Harry's parents, John Anderson Truman and Martha E. Young Truman, on their wedding day, 1882

Madge Wallace enrolled her in Miss Dunlap's dancing classes, attended by children from the town's most important families.

The story is told that one afternoon, thirteen-year-old Bess, wearing a ruffled dress and new patent leather shoes, was sidetracked on her way to dancing class. Her brother Frank needed her to pinch-hit on his baseball team in the ninth inning. His team was behind by three runs until Bess stepped up to the plate, swung, and produced a grand slam home run to win the game. She usually played third base on her brothers' team because she could throw the ball all the way to first base.

Bess was the only girl in town who could whistle through her teeth like a boy. She often used this skill to summon her brothers home and to invite her friends over for ice cream. One of these friends was Mary Paxton, her next-door neighbor. They formed a club, which met after school in

A 1901 picture of Bess Wallace (left) and her friend Mary Paxton

15

Harry S. Truman as a fifteen-year-old high school student

Harry's cousins Nellie (left) and Mary Ethel Noland

Grandfather Gates's barn. There, the girls and their classmates put on plays and charged admission. Bess, the manager, donated the money they earned to charity.

Mary's and Bess's younger brothers frequently got into fights. With Mary at her side, Bess braved flying fists and kicking legs to separate the youngsters. She warned them to "behave or else." When Bess was fourteen, Madge Wallace placed her in charge of her brothers and left on a vacation. Bess easily handled the responsibility of shopping and managing her brothers.

In high school, Harry Truman was not part of Bess's circle of friends. She received invitations to dances, hayrides, and parties almost every weekend while he spent his free time at odd jobs to help support his family. She never considered him more than a schoolmate. They would meet after school to study Latin at the home of his cousins Mary Ethel and Nellie Noland, who lived across the street from the Wallaces.

Although she was an excellent student, Bess did not go on to college as some of her friends did. Her father did

Bess Wallace at her high-school graduation in 1901

not have the money to send her because he was a financial failure. David Wallace even had to borrow money from his father-in-law to pay his taxes. His wife Madge, however, insisted on maintaining a luxurious lifestyle. She did not seem to understand how desperate their monetary situation was. Like many women of her generation, she believed that it was not a wife's place to discuss a man's business or his income with him. Unable to earn more money or to cut his expenses, David began drink-

The Independence High School class of 1901 included Harry Truman (back row, fourth from left) and Bess Wallace (second row, far right).

Madge, Fred, Frank, and Bess Wallace (seated left to right) and Madge's mother, Elizabeth Gates (standing), on one of the family's Colorado trips

This group in the backyard of the Gates-Wallace home includes (left to right) David Wallace, Mary Ethel Noland, Nellie Noland, Frank Wallace, Bess Wallace, George Wallace, and William Boger.

ing heavily with some of his political cronies. On occasion, Bess and her brothers saw him carried home because he was too drunk to manage by himself.

During the summer of 1902, Madge took her children to Colorado Springs for a vacation while David tried to stop drinking. When they returned, he seemed much better. He was even able to help the Paxton family when Mary's mother, a long-time invalid, died of lung disease in May 1903. However, at daybreak on June 18, while the rest of his family slept, David walked into the bathroom, put a gun to his head, and pulled the trigger. Bess awoke to hear her brother Frank shout, "Papa's shot himself!" Mary Paxton rushed next door to comfort Bess. She found her striding in back of the house with her fists clenched. Each having lost a beloved parent, the two girls consoled each other.

In those days, suicide was treated as a weakness of character, a sin, and a scandal. The local newspaper gave a glowing tribute to David Wallace, but it also contained a gruesome account of his death. The reporter asked, "Why should such a man take his own life?" Bess was horrified by the newspaper articles. Madge Wallace collapsed, unable to endure the disgrace of David's suicide and her discovery of the debts he owed. Madge's parents decided that she and her children should leave town for a while and sent them to Colorado Springs. They stayed for a year. It is difficult to know what Bess was thinking during that year because no letters from this time in her life have survived.

In 1905, when the Wallace family returned to Independence, they lived with Madge's parents at 219 North Delaware Street, a three-story, fourteen-room frame house with wide porches in the front and on the sides. Bess thought of this house as home for the rest of her life.

Grandfather Gates sent twenty-year-old Bess to Barstow, a girls' finishing school in Kansas City. She was a good student and an outstanding

The Gates-Wallace home at 219 North Delaware Street, Independence, Missouri

basketball player. This time, she did not go on to college because her mother needed her. Madge had become increasingly isolated and withdrawn. She depended on Bess to take charge of the Wallace boys and to be her companion. Bess dutifully took on these responsibilities, never dreaming that she would become Mrs. Harry S. Truman someday.

*　*　*　*　*　*　*　*　*　*　*　*　*　*

CHAPTER TWO

Becoming Mrs. Harry S. Truman

"She set the style; she was always the leader of our crowd," Mary Paxton said about her friend Bess. Bess threw herself into activities. She set up a bridge club among her card-playing friends and became an active member of the Needlework Guild, which sewed clothing for the needy. Horseback riding, long walks, fishing, and tennis were her favorite pastimes. She also enjoyed driving around town in her grandfather's Studebaker, the first car of its type in Independence. She had plenty of dates, but she did not seem especially eager to marry, and Madge was not prepared to part with her.

This picture of Bess (right) on horseback with friends Laura and Agnes Salisbury (left and middle) was taken in the early 1900s.

During the summer of 1910, Bess was reunited with high school classmate Harry Truman. He showed up on the doorstep of her grandfather's house to return a cake plate loaned to his cousins, the Noland sisters. He and Bess had not seen each other for nine years. After high school, Harry had worked at a Kansas City bank before becoming a farmer, in partnership with his father. He had grown into a sturdy, muscular, healthy-looking young man. She was still the golden-haired, blue-eyed girl of his dreams.

It was difficult for Harry and Bess to get to know each other better. Harry had to work long hours. Although he lived only 15 miles (24 km) away from Bess, unreliable train and streetcar schedules made the trip long and complicated. In 1914, he solved the problem by buying a sec-

Harry in 1908 wearing a derby on his head and a Masonic pin in his lapel

ond-hand car. Phone calls presented another problem. Harry and Bess lacked privacy because the farm was on a party line, connecting a number of families who might listen in on their conversations. This is why the young couple constantly wrote to each other, a practice they continued throughout their lives whenever they were apart.

Years later, Harry found Bess destroying some of those letters. "Bess, you oughtn't do that," he scolded. "Why not? I've read them several times," she replied. "But think of history!" he insisted. "I have!" she explained. Nevertheless, most of Harry's early letters to Bess have survived but very few of hers to him. In his, he discussed the books he read, his favorite music, and the daily details of farm life. His honesty and humor as well as his optimism, his belief that things would get better, impressed Bess. She was a pessimist, seeing life as gloomy and filled with trouble.

When they dated, Harry often took Bess to Kansas City, where they attended light operas, stage plays, and silent movies, the latest entertainment craze. In 1912, Harry escorted Bess to hear William Jennings Bryan, the famous orator of the Democratic party. He was giving a campaign speech for presidential candidate Woodrow Wilson. Bess had been reluctant to go. Perhaps she associated politics with her father's downfall and wanted nothing to do with it. This may have been why she did not support the movement to give women

Silence is Golden

★ ★

It is hard to believe that the simple silent movies Bess and Harry enjoyed on their dates were forerunners of today's multimillion-dollar blockbusters. Indeed, the "flickers" as the first movies were sometimes called, captured the imagination of America. Despite their flickering images, bad acting, and awkward plots, moving pictures fascinated early viewers. These short, one-reel comedies, travelogs, and dramas cost about $500 to make and took only a few days to film. In the theater, a live organist or a mechanical piano accompanied the show with dramatic music to enhance the plot. Words of explanation or dialogue often appeared on the screen. By 1910, ten thousand silent movie theaters operated coast to coast drawing a total weekly audience of ten million people, each of whom paid five cents to see the show. As the years went by, silent films grew longer and more sophisticated. Finally, in 1927, the first "talkie," a film called *The Jazz Singer*, marked the end of the golden age of silent films.

When Bess and Harry were dating, they often went to the Royal Theatre in Kansas City (right) where they saw the latest silent movies.

24

William Jennings Bryan (1860–1925)

✬ ✬ ✬ ✬ ✬ ✬ ✬ ✬ ✬ ✬ ✬ ✬ ✬ ✬ ✬ ✬ ✬ ✬ ✬ ✬

Born in Salem, Illinois, William Jenning Bryan forged a long career in politics. His tall good looks and booming voice made Bryan an engaging and popular speaker.

Serving as a Nebraska congressman from 1890 to 1894, he supported the use of silver instead of gold as a new monetary standard for the country. This would make more money available to those hurt by the farm depression of the 1880s and 1890s and help them pay back their loans. When not running for president (he ran and lost three times), he edited the *Omaha World-Herald* and lectured on government reforms. He was the first politician to use the railroads extensively in his campaigning. Bryan resigned as secretary of state under President Wilson because he did not want the United States to enter World War I. At the end of his career, his belief in the Bible's story of creation made him a star

William Jennings Bryan

witness against John Scopes, a teacher in Tennessee who had broken the law by teaching evolution. Scopes's attorney, the famous Clarence Darrow, humiliated Bryan on the stand. While teacher Scopes got off with only a token fine, Bryan, exhausted by his efforts, died a few days later.

Harry Truman in 1914

voting rights. Most of her friends did not favor female suffrage either, and in 1914, Missourians defeated a proposal to have women vote in state and local elections.

There were a number of obstacles to a marriage between Harry and Bess. The main roadblock was Bess herself. When Harry proposed by letter in 1911, she rejected him but agreed to remain his friend. Finally, in November 1913, she told him that if she were

Harry on a horse at the Grandview farm in his uniform as a corporal of the Missouri National Guard

This April 6, 1917, New York Journal *headline announced the declaration of World War I.*

ever to marry anyone, it would be he. Money was another problem. Harry Truman simply could not afford to take a wife. To make matters worse, in November 1914, his father died, saddling him with a legacy of debts and the responsibility for his mother and sister. To earn money, he tried land sales, mining, and the oil business without success.

Predictably, Madge Wallace objected to Bess seeing Harry. She felt that as a farmer, he was not her daughter's social equal. Bess had dated young men from important Independence families and found them dull. Unlike her mother, she did not judge people by their wealth or background and continued to go out with Harry. She knew that Madge would find fault with any young man who came to call because she wanted Bess to remain single and take care of her. Nevertheless, in 1917, Bess demanded that her mother announce her engagement in the newspapers.

This time Harry backed off. He had become a soldier. On April 6, 1917, the United States declared war against the Central Powers (Germany and Austria-Hungary) and entered World War I on the side of the Allied Powers (England, France, and Russia). Harry could have been excused from military duty because of his poor vision and his occupation as a farmer. Instead, he decided to serve his country by re-enrolling in the Missouri National Guard, which he had belonged to from 1905 to 1911.

He asked Bess to postpone wedding plans until the war was over. Because

World War I: Fast Facts

WHAT: The "Great War," the "War to End All Wars," the first truly global conflict

WHEN: 1914–1918

WHO: The Central European Powers, including Austria-Hungary and Germany, opposed the Allied Powers, including Britain, France, and Russia. The United States entered the war on the Allied side in 1917.

WHERE: The Central Powers invaded Serbia, Romania, Russia, Belgium, France, and Italy. Fighting extended into the Atlantic Ocean and the Mediterranean Sea.

WHY: European disputes over land, economics, religion, and leadership boiled over in 1914 when Austrian archduke Francis Ferdinand was assassinated on a visit to Serbia. Austria declared war on Serbia, and other European nations joined in. The United States got involved largely because German submarine warfare disrupted commerce in the North Atlantic Ocean.

OUTCOME: The Central Powers fell to the Allied Powers in 1918, and a peace treaty was signed on November 11. The map of Europe was redrawn and the League of Nations was founded to settle international disputes. Ten million soldiers, including 116,500 Americans, had died.

he was aware of the Allied casualty rates, he wrote to her, "I don't think it would be right for me to ask you to tie yourself to a prospective cripple." They exchanged photographs before Harry was shipped overseas. On the back of the picture she sent him, she wrote, "Dear Harry, May this photograph bring you safely home from France—Bess."

While Captain Harry Truman was in France commanding Battery D of the 129th Field Artillery, Bess kept busy. She attended meetings of the Woman's Auxiliary of the 129th Reg-

Harry Truman, at the age of nineteen, was a member of the Missouri National Guard.

Captain Harry S. Truman (second from left) with others in France in 1919

A Washington, D.C., crowd holding newspapers with headlines announcing the end of World War I

iment with the wives and fiancées of Harry's unit. She volunteered to sell Liberty bonds, which were bought by citizens as a loan to the federal government to help pay for the war. In 1918, Bess also served on a welcoming committee for soldiers visiting from nearby army bases. Like many other women facing wartime shortages of flour and sugar, she learned how to cook without those ingredients. She

constantly had to calm Madge, who feared her sons would be drafted. Somehow she also found time to visit Harry's mother and to reply to each of Harry's frequent letters.

The year 1918 was one of mixed blessings for Bess. In June, her beloved Grandfather Gates died. Then on November 11, Bess and her friends joined their neighbors in celebrating the end of World War I. Later that

"Knit Your Bit"

★ ★ ★ ★ ★ ★ ★ ★ ★ ★ ★ ★ ★ ★ ★ ★ ★ ★ ★

As the country entered World War I, Americans pitched in as Bess did to support the war effort. Many volunteered to serve soldiers on their way to Europe at makeshift canteens in railroad stations. To conserve supplies, food, and energy, Americans endured endless rationing, cutting back on everything from coal to butter. Patriotic citizens observed "heatless, meatless, and wheatless" days. Since Germany led the world in producing fabric dyes, color disappeared from American clothing. Steel went into guns and tanks instead of into women's corsets. Women wore lower heels in an effort to provide leather for military harnesses and belts. Cloth was conserved by eliminating outside pockets on men's suits. Youngsters hooted at anyone thoughtless enough to drive their cars on gasless Sundays, while diligent motorists hitched horses to the bumpers of their cars.

New York City celebrated the surrender of Germany on Armistice Day, November 11, 1918, with a huge ticker-tape parade.

Washington, D.C., the nation's capital, held a huge Armistice Day parade on November 11, 1918, to celebrate the World War I victory.

month, she came down with influenza. For weeks, she ran a high fever and sometimes lost consciousness. Because antibiotics and preventive vaccines had not yet been developed, the flu epidemic of 1918 was devastating. The disease spread to 46 states and took between 400,000 and 500,000 lives. In January, Bess was finally well enough to return to her activities.

With Harry still overseas, Bess made her wedding plans by mail. In the earliest of her letters to survive, she wrote, "You may invite the entire 35th Division to your wedding if you want. I guess it's going to be yours as well as mine."

On June 28, 1919, seven weeks after he was discharged from service, the thirty-four-year-old captain mar-

A June 1918 view of Chicago's Michigan Avenue, where Harry and Bess spent part of their honeymoon just a year later

ried his thirty-three-year-old bride in a tiny church near the Wallace home. Some of his military buddies as well as their old friends and family members attended the wedding. Punch and ice cream were served at the reception on the lawn of 219 North Delaware Street. Then the newlyweds drove off to spend their honeymoon in Chicago, Illinois, and Detroit and Port Huron, Michigan. Bess never expected that in a few years, Harry would run for public office and she would become a politician's wife.

✶　✶　✶　✶　✶　✶　✶　✶　✶　✶　✶　✶　✶　✶　✶

CHAPTER THREE

Learning to Be a Politician's Wife

* * * * * * * * * * * * * * * * *

"I'd take the books home and Mrs. Truman would help me with them," Harry explained. In 1919, Harry and army buddy Eddie Jacobson opened a men's clothing store in Kansas City. At night, Bess recorded in an account book the store's sales receipts and expense slips. Unlike her mother, Bess took an active interest in her husband's career and shared his hopes and fears. He could confide in her and depend on her. By 1922, the store closed because the economy had slowed down, leaving people with less spending money.

Bess soon became the wife of a local politician. With the backing of Western Missouri's Democratic

* * * * * * * * * * * * * * * * *

Harry (left front) and others pose in the men's clothing store in which Harry was a partner between 1919 and 1922.

The exterior of the men's clothing store in Kansas City

Missouri Democratic party boss Thomas J. Pendergast

party boss Tom Pendergast, Harry ran for public office. Bosses were politicians who traded political favors for money and votes to keep their own political organizations in power. During Harry's campaign, Bess suffered a failed pregnancy, which kept her at home. Her friends rang doorbells, asking people to vote for him. He was elected Jackson County judge in 1922. This was the Missouri equivalent of a county commissioner, an official who

supervised road building and the construction and maintenance of public buildings.

The Trumans were living with Madge Wallace at 219 North Delaware Street, which helped them save money and gave Madge the comfort of Bess's company. Life with Madge was a mixed blessing for the Trumans, however. She still did not approve of her daughter's husband or his choice of career. She was heard to say, "Mr. Truman isn't a real judge! He can't marry anybody or sentence a robber caught in the act." It was a relief for Harry Truman to have an informal Sunday lunch with Mamma Truman at the farm. Unlike Madge Wallace, Harry's mother did not require her guests to make small talk and dress up for meals.

Bess ignored her mother's complaints about the constant phone calls and visits from local Missourians wanting Harry to fix their roads or find them a job. She even handled matters for Harry when he spent two weeks each summer on active duty with the Missouri National Guard. During his stay in military camp, they wrote to each other daily. She briefed him on local political doings and clipped newspaper articles that would interest him. This became the pattern for their lives whenever they were apart. At first, Bess resented her husband's absences. However, she soon recognized that the two-week military exercises gave him relief from tension headaches, brought on by the stress of his job.

On February 17, 1924, Bess gave birth to Mary Margaret, better known by her middle name. Later that year, with Republicans winning nationwide, Harry failed to be reelected, his only political defeat. Bess suggested that he attend law school at night, but after two years, he found himself too busy to continue. Harry took a number of different jobs to support his family until he was elected presiding judge, or chief commissioner, in 1926.

When Harry left on road-inspection trips in Missouri and out of state, Bess wrote to him about local politics and family news. She also checked his office to make sure his staff was working. Bess was not able join her husband on his travels. Madge had become increasingly dependent on her, and Margaret was a sickly child. In 1930, after someone attempted to kidnap Margaret, Bess walked her to

Margaret Truman as an eighteen-month-old in the summer of 1926

Presiding judge Harry S. Truman (center) in 1927

and from school every day. "I'm taking no chances," she said. Because she was home more consistently, Bess became the family disciplinarian, occasionally spanking Margaret for misbehavior. Harry enjoyed spoiling his little girl.

After the stock market crashed in 1929, Harry was fortunate to be an officeholder. The nation's economy had ground to a standstill. What was called the Great Depression put almost 13 million Americans out of work. At Bess's request, Harry found jobs for two of her brothers. George became the superintendent of the Jackson County highway department, a job he held for the rest of his life. Fred, an architect, worked on the construction of a new hospital. Her brothers' heavy drinking caused difficulties for Harry and worried Bess. George finally overcame his problem, but Fred did not.

In 1934, to Bess's surprise, Boss Pendergast picked Harry to run for the United States Senate. She made sev-

Top: Margaret on a swing with her doll in the summer of 1928
Bottom: Margaret with her trike in the fall of 1928

The Crash of 1929

✭ ✭

In the fall of 1929, the American economy appeared hale and hearty. Investors in the stock market could hardly believe their good fortune as the value of their stocks shot higher and higher. Americans everywhere followed the market with great excitement as it soared. More and more people began to speculate, or buy stocks hoping that their value would increase. Some overextended themselves by borrowing money to buy more stocks. The prospect of easy profits obscured the warning signs that an economic crisis was looming. Most of America's money was concentrated in the hands of a wealthy few. The prices for farm products fell and farmers lost money. Rural banks failed because farmers couldn't pay off their loans. Ordinary consumers didn't make enough money to buy all the goods that businesses were producing. Finally, disaster struck when the stock market "crashed." Investors who had borrowed money began to sell their stocks to cover their debts. Stock prices nose-dived. On October 29, 1929, known as Black Tuesday, panicked investors sold more than 16 million shares of stock for much less than they had paid. Fortunes disappeared in minutes. The crash ruined banks, businesses, and individuals and triggered the worst depression in American history.

During the depression, many homeless and unemployed men stood in a Kansas City soup line (left) and others ate Christmas dinner at a New York City soup kitchen (right).

Margaret (left, at the age of ten) joined her parents, Bess (center) and Harry Truman, at a Democratic dinner when Harry was senator-elect in 1934.

eral campaign appearances with her husband but refused to speak in public. She explained to his cousin Ethel Noland, "A woman's place in public is to sit beside her husband, be silent, and be sure her hat is on straight." In the 1930s, most women would have agreed with her.

During the campaign, Bess was angry and upset when the newspapers falsely accused Harry of corruption because of his ties to Boss Pendergast.

Bess knew her husband had never taken a bribe. As a judge, he had awarded road construction contracts to the most qualified firms; these were not necessarily the companies Pendergast recommended. At her prompting, a newspaper editor, related to the Wallace family, ran a series of articles emphasizing Harry's clean record.

After he won, Bess told a reporter, "Of course, I'm thrilled to be going to Washington, but I have spent all my

life here on Delaware Street and it will be a change." She wasn't thrilled at all to be leaving her family and friends. To her relief, however, she discovered that the nation's capital was not the impersonal East Coast big city she dreaded but a hospitable small southern town. She quickly settled into the apartment Harry had found and enrolled Margaret in Gunston Hall, a private school for girls. Then she joined the Congressional Club where she met other lawmakers' wives. She said, "I found the Senate women only too glad to talk of household matters

Senator-elect Harry S. Truman at his desk in 1934

Mrs. John Nance Garner, wife of the vice president (third from left), hosts the wives of the new U.S. senators at the first Ladies Luncheon, of which she was president. Bess Truman is second from left.

and family questions, as women will in any part of the world." She also visited Harry's office regularly and took an interest in the personal lives of his staff—especially if their conduct reflected poorly on him.

To economize, Bess did the housework, shopped for food, and prepared meals herself. The Trumans, however, entertained their guests at restaurants because Bess did not enjoy cooking for dinner parties. She soon grew dissatisfied with the quality and cost of laundry service in the capital and sent the family's clothing by mail to Kansas City to be cleaned. In addition to her chores, she wrote home daily, sending special delivery letters to her mother for arrival on Sundays.

Bess was torn between her husband and her mother and spent six months of every year in Independence and six in the nation's capital. When the Trumans were apart, she continued to send Harry clippings from the local papers and political gossip. In time, she realized that newspaper attacks on her husband were not personal but

Bess (left), Margaret, and Harry at their Independence home in 1940 after Harry's reelction to the U.S. Senate

merely part of the game of politics. From Washington, Harry sent her the latest information, including the *Congressional Record*, containing the lawmakers' debates. He used her as a sounding board for his decisions. Through their correspondence, she raised questions that got him to think out his views more carefully. He went on to defend President Franklin D. Roosevelt's New Deal, a series of government programs to help the nation recover from the Great Depression.

Bess encouraged Harry to run for reelection in 1940. She worked behind the scenes, helping him to decide which members of his staff should join him on the campaign trail. As usual, when he was in Washington, she served as his eyes and ears in Missouri. Harry fought off challenges from Democratic state politicians who wanted to take his place. Short on funds, he mounted a grassroots campaign, appealing to ordinary citizens, and won.

In 1942, Senator Harry S. Truman (center), chairman of the Truman Committee, and fellow senators inspected this bomber assembly line at the Glenn L. Martin plant in Baltimore.

In 1941, at the beginning of her husband's second term, Bess decided to remain in Washington, going home just for vacations. World War II was already in its second year. Among the Allies, France, Belgium, Holland, and Norway had fallen, leaving Britain and the Soviet Union at the mercy of the Axis powers: Germany, Italy, and

Japan. Congress was meeting in continuous session as the nation rearmed and arranged to supply the Allies.

Meanwhile, Truman became chairman of the Senate Special Committee to Investigate the National Defense Program. The Truman Committee, as it was called, had been formed in February to expose waste and corruption

World War II: Fast Facts

WHAT: The second great global conflict

WHEN: 1939–1945

WHO: The Axis Powers, including Germany, Italy, and Japan, opposed the Allies, including Britain, France, and the USSR. The United States entered the war on the Allied side in 1941 after Japan bombed the American naval base at Pearl Harbor in Hawaii.

WHERE: Fighting raged throughout the Pacific Ocean and in the Atlantic, as well as from Scandinavia to North Africa, and deep into the Soviet Union.

WHY: Chancellor Adolf Hitler set out to make Germany the most powerful country in the world and began by invading his European neighbors. Japan, Italy, and Germany pledged support to one another in 1940. When the United States declared war on Japan after the attack on Pearl Harbor in 1941, Germany and Italy declared war on the United States.

OUTCOME: The war ended in stages. Germany surrendered in May 1945. Japan surrendered after the United States dropped two atomic bombs there in August. More than 400,000 American troops died in battle; about 17 million on both sides perished.

in the defense industries. Harry put his wife on the government payroll to serve as a researcher and secretary to the committee. Harry had confidence in Bess's abilities. She had been greeting delegations of Missourians and handling his routine correspondence for years. To Republican complaints, Harry replied, "She earns every cent of it. I never make a speech without going over it with her . . . not one of these reports [of the committee] has been issued without going through her hands."

The Japanese surprise attack on Pearl Harbor on December 7, 1941, caught Senator Truman resting in Columbia, Missouri, after an exhausting inspection tour of defense plants. Bess heard about the bombing on the radio and phoned him to return to Washington. He arrived just in time to cast his vote for a declaration of war against Japan. Fortunately, the Tru-

President Franklin Delano Roosevelt (FDR) after signing the declaration of war against Japan

Pearl Harbor

✳ ✳

Described by President Franklin D. Roosevelt as "a date which will live in infamy," December 7, 1941, dawned peacefully enough over the Hawaiian island of Oahu. Then, at 7:55 A.M., Japan's surprise attack on the American naval base at Pearl Harbor shattered the morning. The first wave of 185 planes included high-level bombers, torpedo bombers, dive-bombers, and fighters. Then 170 more planes pounded the base again. In two hours, the attack crippled the U.S. Pacific fleet resting at dock and anchor. Eight battleships sank. Light cruisers, destroyers, auxiliary ships, and aircraft were destroyed or seriously damaged. The next day, Congress declared war on Japan, and the United States entered World War II. As the smoke cleared, the fate of the USS *Arizona* proved the most tragic with the loss of 1,102 crewmen. Its rusting hulk rests on the harbor's bottom to this day, oil still surfacing from its engines. A memorial to the 2,400 Americans killed at Pearl Harbor spans, without touching, the midsection of the great sunken ship.

Pearl Harbor as it looked moments after the December 7, 1941, attack by Japanese aircraft

FDR delivering his declaration of war speech before a joint session of Congress

The Trumans are shown in the kitchen of their Washington, D.C., apartment in April 1942

mans did not become victims of the housing shortage in wartime Washington, D.C. They had already moved into a comfortable rental apartment on Connecticut Avenue where Bess soon had to cope with shortages of food and gasoline.

In 1944, Bess learned that the Democratic party leadership wanted her husband to be Roosevelt's vice president. The work of the Truman Committee had made Harry a nationally respected figure. The president was seeking an unprecedented fourth term in office. (Other American presidents had served no more than two

An April 1942 photograph of Senator Truman working at the desk in his office

Harry and Bess at home in Washington just before Harry's nomination as FDR's running mate

terms.) The Trumans knew that because of Roosevelt's poor health, his next vice president would probably become president.

Bess did not want Harry to be nominated. She enjoyed being a senator's wife. She feared that if her husband became president, he would kill himself with overwork. Doctors had already found him on the verge of collapse from exhaustion, and he had suffered a severe gall bladder attack. Unwilling to give up her privacy, she also wanted to protect herself and Margaret from the newspaper attacks that Eleanor Roosevelt and her children endured. She had thought the matter was closed when Harry committed himself to support another candidate for vice president.

Nevertheless, the national Democratic party leadership, headed by Missourian Robert E. Hannegan, still wanted Harry. When President Roosevelt phoned to persuade him, Harry agreed to be nominated. After the party members chose him as Roosevelt's running mate, the new candidate, his wife, and their daughter were immediately crushed by crowds of

During a hometown reception, Independence mayor Robert T. Sermon (right) and Mrs. Sermon (second from left) congratulate the Truman family on Harry's nomination as candidate for vice president.

well-wishers and photographers. With help from a police escort, they finally reached their waiting car. A furious Bess asked her husband, "Are we going to have to go through this for the rest of our lives?" She valued her privacy more than the honor of being Second Lady of the land, or even First Lady.

Bess, Harry, and Margaret being introduced at a Lamar, Missouri, rally in August 1944

53

CHAPTER FOUR

Serving as First Lady

☆ ☆ ☆ ☆ ☆ ☆ ☆ ☆ ☆ ☆ ☆ ☆ ☆ ☆ ☆

"I'm just getting excited," Bess told reporters at her first and only press conference, held before the election of 1944. While Harry campaigned around the nation, she phoned him with advice. Bess insisted that he stop participating in such undignified, silly stunts as cow-milking contests and Indian war dances. Meanwhile, she brought her ailing mother to Washington to live in the Trumans' Connecticut Avenue apartment.

As the new Second Lady of the land, Bess attended so many social functions in the capital that she complained, "I've begun thinking that the ideal wife of a vice president should be skeleton-thin." By this time,

☆ ☆ ☆ ☆ ☆ ☆ ☆ ☆ ☆ ☆ ☆ ☆ ☆ ☆ ☆

Harry Truman and Franklin Roosevelt discussing campaign strategy in 1944

Harry Truman casting his vote in the 1944 presidential election

56

*Left to right: Margaret, Bess, and Harry Truman
setting off for Harry's inauguration as vice president*

A headline on the front page of The New York
Times *announces the death of the president.*

Bess had become a rather stocky woman, known for wearing sensible suits and no-nonsense hats. Her blonde curly hair had turned to gray. Harry commented proudly, "She looks exactly as a woman her age should look."

On April 12, 1945, after only 82 days as the vice president's wife, Bess became First Lady. She burst into tears when Harry phoned to inform her that the president had died. She and Margaret quickly joined him at the White House where they paid their respects to Mrs. Roosevelt. Bess looked grim as she watched Harry take the presidential oath of office.

She could not sleep that night. In addition to worrying about her hus-

Harry S. Truman taking the oath of office as president on April 12, 1945, with Bess (center) and Margaret (right) accompanying him

President Truman arrives at the White House at 9:00 A.M. on April 13, 1945, the morning after he became president of the Untied States.

A Tough Act to Follow

✫ ✫

It's no wonder Bess Truman was nervous about following in Eleanor Roosevelt's footsteps. Upon moving into the White House, Eleanor told a reporter, "There isn't going to be any First Lady. There is just going to be plain, ordinary Mrs. Roosevelt." Eleanor turned out to be neither. She traveled and campaigned tirelessly for human rights, equality for women and blacks, and humanitarian causes. While Franklin Roosevelt was president in the 1930s and 1940s, she covered thousands of miles a year, visiting the coal mines of Pennsylvania and the cornfields of the Midwest. During World War II, she took a five-week trip to visit wounded soldiers in the South Pacific. After Franklin Roosevelt's death, President Truman appointed Eleanor to the United Nations, where she worked very hard for war refugees. In 1952, she accepted an invitation of India's prime minister and visited not only that  country but managed to "drop in" on the leaders of Lebanon, Syria, Jordan, and Pakistan. She visited Japan, meeting Emperor Hirohito and his wife, the Empress Nagako. She saw firsthand the devastation at Hiroshima, where Americans had dropped the atom bomb in 1945. In 1957, Eleanor traveled throughout the Soviet Union, ending her trip with a visit to Premier Nikita Khrushchev, whom she interviewed for the *New York Post*. Eleanor's remarkable career has served as an inspiration for women and girls the world over.

*President Franklin Delano
Roosevelt's funeral procession
on April 14, 1945*

*Bess (left), Harry (center), and
Margaret Truman (right)
attending Roosevelt's funeral
services at the Roosevelt estate
in Hyde Park, New York*

The Trumans lived in Blair House (above) until May 7, 1945.

band, she admitted, "I was very apprehensive. The country was used to Eleanor Roosevelt. I couldn't possibly be anything like her." Although Eleanor had held frequent press conferences with women reporters, Bess decided to cancel hers at the last minute. "I am not the one who is elected. I have nothing to say to the public," she explained to the disappointed journalists. She wanted her

privacy and persisted in answering their questions with a brisk, "No comment."

Shortly after attending Roosevelt's funeral, the Trumans moved into Blair House, across the street from the White House, to spare their apartment-house neighbors the disruption of secret service surveillance and crowds of well-wishers. The move gave Mrs. Roosevelt time to pack up and leave the Executive Mansion. The Trumans occupied the White House on May 7, 1945, the day before celebrations of Harry's sixty-first birthday and V-E (Victory in Europe) Day, marking the surrender of Germany.

Bess was determined to maintain her normal family routine in the White House, but Mrs. Henrietta Nesbitt, the Executive Mansion's housekeeper, was uncooperative. Whenever Bess made suggestions, the housekeeper insisted, "This isn't the way Mrs. Roosevelt did it." She even ignored the Trumans' frequent requests to stop serving brussel sprouts at meals. She defied the new First Lady for the last time when Bess asked

Because Henrietta Nesbitt, who had been the Executive Mansion housekeeper during the Roosevelt Administration, was set in her ways and would not accede to the Trumans' wishes, Bess finally had to have her fired.

Reathel Odum, Bess's personal secretary

Charles G. Ross, Harry's press secretary

for some butter to bring to her Washington bridge club. Mrs. Nesbitt wouldn't give it to her, claiming that the White House had almost used up its rationing stamps. (During wartime, rationing was used to limit the amount of scarce supplies American families could use.) Mrs. Nesbitt was fired. Despite that unfortunate experience, the Trumans genuinely cared about the household servants. Bess and Harry soon learned everyone's names. They even introduced the staff to their visitors, something their predecessors did not do.

During a typical day as First Lady, Bess had breakfast with her husband and daughter. Then she went to her office on the second floor to look over her appointment schedule and go over her mail with Reathel Odum, her personal secretary, and Edith Helm, her social secretary. Wearing a simple house dress, she reviewed White House expenses with J. B. West, soon to become chief usher, the administrative official in charge of running the White House. Bess was determined to account for every penny spent at the White House. She willingly did the bookkeeping and carefully supervised expenditures even after Congress voted the president an expense account of $50,000 and an allowance to feed the White House help. Unlike other presidential families, the Trumans were not independently wealthy.

After lunch with Harry, Bess spent time with her invalid mother before attending official afternoon receptions. If none were scheduled, she read a mystery novel or listened to a baseball game on the radio. Afterward, Bess joined Harry and Margaret for an informal dinner, but the waiters wore formal clothes, a White House tradition. The Trumans were even known to flick watermelon seeds at one another at the end of a meal. Until Margaret left for New York to become a concert singer, she lived with her parents.

Bess had a difficult time during her first year as First Lady. She was most unhappy because her political partnership with Harry temporarily dissolved. He did take her suggestion to name their old high school classmate, editor Charlie Ross, to be his press secretary.

The atomic bomb explosion over Nagasaki

The Atomic Age Explodes

✫ ✫ ✫ ✫ ✫ ✫ ✫ ✫ ✫ ✫ ✫ ✫ ✫ ✫ ✫ ✫ ✫ ✫ ✫

Among the government programs unknown to Vice President Harry Truman, one loomed particularly large. President Roosevelt had not told his vice president about the Manhattan Project, the top-secret American attempt to develop an atomic bomb. The United States gathered many of the world's greatest scientists together in secret laboratories to make the bomb before Nazi Germany did. President Truman's decision to drop two of the devastating new weapons on the Japanese cities of Hiroshima and Nagasaki shook the world. Very little was known about atomic energy and the serious illnesses that radiation, a by-product of atomic explosion, could cause. These factors made the bombs, nicknamed "Little Boy" and "Fat Man," much more deadly than their mere explosive power. With two cities instantly destroyed, a badly shaken Japan surrendered unconditionally, ending World War II. It took a year to approximate the number of people killed by the atomic bombs. Studies of Hiroshima suggest that 130,000 or more people died, and a survey of Nagasaki's deaths concluded that approximately 74,000 lives were lost within seconds. Today, survivors and their families still suffer from illnesses and genetic defects caused by the radiation, and the world struggles to prevent the use of atomic weapons ever again.

Yet he did not consult her during the marathon briefings he received shortly after becoming president. Roosevelt had failed to inform him about his plans to end the war or about any of his programs. Harry had a lot of catching up to do. Accustomed to discussing Harry's political decisions with him, Bess felt like an outsider. In his July 1945 letters from Germany, he shared his impressions of meetings with European wartime leaders with her and his decision to drop an atomic bomb on Japan to end the war. When he returned, however, he did not confide in her.

This front page banner headline appeared in the Chicago Daily News on August 14, 1945.

COOLER
Clearing, cooler tonight, low 68. Wednesday fair, cool, much lower humidity, high 78. Sunrise, 5:55; sunset, ...
(Turn to page 26 for official weather report.)

CHICAGO DAILY NEWS

RED STREAK

70TH YEAR—191.
TUESDAY, AUGUST 14, 1945—TWENTY-SIX PAGES. ★ FOUR CENTS

WAR ENDS

Truman Announces Japanese Surrender

Child Reveals Mystery Death

Found Wandering at Dawn, He Leads Way to Body of G.I. Wife

(Picture on Page 4)

The death of a soldier's wife, found half nude in her home, gave police today one of the most baffling mysteries in recent years.

The victim was Mrs. Mildred Bollenbach, 21, pretty, red-haired wife of Pvt. Ray Bollenbach, recently returned from Germany and now stationed at Camp Gruber, Okla., en route to the Pacific.

Her body was discovered in her apartment at 5816 Dorchester av. early today after her 3-year-old son Jimmy was found wandering in the rain just before dawn. Neighbors who recognized him took ...

Chicago Lets Go in Advance

Paper Snowstorm Expresses Gaiety

(Pictures on Back Page)
BY ROBERT FAHERTY.

Official word that the Japanese reply was being transmitted to President Truman touched off another spontaneous celebration—one of many in the last few days—in Chicago's downtown.

But the revived celebrating was not general in the Loop—only certain sections, particularly the western area ...

Fighting Goes On As World Waits

As the world waited today for Washington's official announcement of the Japanese surrender.

Latest Bulletins

GUAM—(UP)—The entire 20th Air Force has been ordered to hit Japan with maximum B-29 blows to shatter any Jap hopes of stalling for time while they debate peace terms.

By the United Press.

Jap radio stations have begun to contact all Jap ships at sea, American Broadcasting Co. monitors reported today. It was recalled that Germany similarly contacted her ships at sea before surrendering to the Western Allies.

LONDON—(UP)—An Exchange Telegraph dispatch reported today that Radio Tokyo had announced the withdrawal of Japanese forces from southeastern Burma.

PARIS—(UP)—Andre le Troquer, president of ...

Hirohito Gives His Decision

Domei Reveals Tokyo Reaction

By the Associated Press.
Domei, Japanese news agency, said in a broadcast today that "on Aug. 14, 1945, the imperial decision was granted" and that weeping people had gathered before his palace and "bowed to the very ground" in their shame that their "efforts were not enough."

The broadcast did not say what the Emperor's decision was.

Domei transmitted only about ...

EXTRA
Tokyo Accepts Allied Terms

BULLETIN

WASHINGTON — (AP) — President Truman announced at 6:00 p.m. (Chicago time) tonight Japanese acceptance of surrender terms.

★ ★ ★

WASHINGTON—(UP)—Japan's reply to Allied ...

Crowds celebrating on the White House lawn on August 14, 1945, V-J Day (Victory over Japan Day)

66

When Bess tried to christen this navy hospital evacuation plane in May 1945, the champagne bottle would not break (left), so a naval officer finally hit the bottle with a hammer (right).

A 1945 photo of the Trumans at home in Independence, Missouri, the "Summer White House"

Then she was embarrassed when she tried to christen a navy hospital evacuation plane. She swung a bottle of champagne against the side of the plane seven times, but it refused to break. Finally, a naval officer hit the bottle with a hammer. At dinner, when Harry heard of her misadventure, he teased, "And I always thought you had a strong right arm from playing tennis." She was not amused.

Bess faced a more difficult challenge in October when the Daughters of the American Revolution (DAR) invited her to tea at Constitution

67

When Bess decided to attend a DAR tea (right), she incurred the wrath of Congressman Adam Clayton Powell Jr.

Congressman Adam Clayton Powell Jr. objected to Bess's decision to attend a DAR tea.

Hall. Black Congressman Adam Clayton Powell Jr. asked her not to attend. He explained that the DAR had refused to let his wife, pianist Hazel Scott, perform in the hall because of her race. He reminded Bess that Eleanor Roosevelt had resigned from the DAR to protest its similar treatment of black opera star Marian Anderson. Bess replied that she would go ahead with her plans. They were made before the controversy over Hazel Scott arose. She explained, "In my opinion, the acceptance of the hospitality is not related to the merits of the issue." Harry supported his wife's stand.

The angry congressman called her "the Last Lady" of the land. As a result, Powell was not welcome at the White House. Like many white people of their generation, neither Harry nor Bess ever socialized with blacks. They had grown up in a segregated Missouri town. Yet President Harry Truman went on to back civil rights for blacks and to integrate the armed services of the United States.

Because she was still excluded from his political decisions, Bess did not welcome Harry when he returned to Independence for the Christmas holidays. She snapped at him, "As far as I'm concerned, you might as well have stayed in Washington." After this reprimand, they soon became a team again. In fact, after Harry left office, he told a reporter that Bess was "a full partner in all my transactions—politically and otherwise." Among the subjects they discussed were Harry's decision to give aid to war-torn Europe through the 1947 Marshall Plan, and

Pianist Hazel Scott

The Trumans in Independence at Christmas 1946

The Korean War: Fast Facts

WHAT: Conflict between Communist North Korea and the constitutional republic of South Korea

WHEN: 1950–1953

WHO: The Soviet Union and Communist China backed North Korea. The United States, along with a multinational UN force, supported South Korea.

WHERE: At the end of World War II, the Korean peninsula was divided into North Korea and South Korea at the 38th parallel. Fighting ranged up and down the peninsula but eventually concentrated along the boundary line.

WHY: When North Korea invaded South Korea, the United States feared a communist takeover. The United Nations condemned North Korea, and member nations mounted a "police action" (never technically a war) to stop the invasion. A Chinese counterattack drove UN forces out of North Korea in December 1950 and led to a standoff around the 38th parallel.

OUTCOME: An armistice agreement was finally signed on July 27, 1953. The conflict failed to reunite the divided nation. The invasion had been turned back at great cost: more than 3.8 million people from both sides were killed, wounded, or went missing during the Korean War.

to help the Republic of South Korea repel an invasion from Communist-run North Korea by sending American troops to Asia in 1950. (Communism is a set of ideas emphasizing state ownership of the economy in the name of the people, practiced by the former Soviet Union, now Russia, and other nations then under its control.)

"Her judgment was always good," Harry explained. Bess listened and questioned him as she had always done, so that his own thinking became clearer. Bess also tried to support his programs. For example, in 1946, she launched a Spanish class at the White House to promote Inter-American relations. She invited the wives of government officials to join her. For their "graduation," they prepared a Spanish lunch in the White House kitchen.

As First Lady, Bess was also President Harry Truman's official hostess. Although she much preferred to entertain informally, she was gracious

Bess Truman (front row, second from right) organized a Spanish class at the White House for wives of government officials.

71

Harry (left), Bess, and Margaret (partially hidden) greet members of the American Newspaper Women's Club during a White House reception.

and dignified at ceremonial functions. In the fall of 1946, the Trumans launched the social season at the White House. Bess had to shake hands with more than 4,100 guests. When asked how she did it, she commented, "I have a strong tennis arm." Despite all the important people she met, Bess much preferred entertaining her bridge club from Independence at the White House. She made sure that they ate in the State Dining Room and were treated as VIPs (very important people). To Bess, they were.

Members of her Independence, Missouri, bridge club were guests of First Lady Bess Truman (fifth from right) at the White House in May 1946.

Bess supported her husband when he decided to run for the presidency in 1948. Nobody, least of all Bess, expected Harry to defeat his Republican opponent Governor Thomas E. Dewey of New York, but she was part of the group that planned his strategy. Harry traveled around the country by train giving speeches from the rear platform. On these railroad trips, Bess went over his speeches, saw that he ate and rested, and sewed on loose coat buttons. Harry often introduced Bess as the "Boss," and Margaret as "the one who bosses the boss." Bess tolerated these introductions even though she disliked them. They delighted Harry's small-town audiences. They, too, were "bossed" by strong-willed wives who would rarely express an opinion in public but would certainly make their views

New York Governor Thomas E. Dewey was Truman's opponent in the presidential election of 1948.

known to their husbands in private. On January 20, 1949, Bess proudly watched Harry being sworn in as president in his own right. His inaugural speech was the first to be carried on television.

Harry consulted her on all his speeches. She waged a losing battle to get him to clean up his blunt language. Members of the White House staff constantly heard her telling him, "You didn't have to say that." The story is told that one of Bess's friends complained that her husband wouldn't say "fertilizer" instead of "manure." Bess replied, "And I've been trying to get Harry to say manure!"

Bess and Harry wave from the Truman campaign train in October 1948. Margaret stands between them.

Crowds gather to hear Harry speak at a campaign stop in Richmond, Indiana.

Before the election results were final, the Chicago Daily Tribune, *assuming mistakenly that Dewey would win the 1948 presidential election, printed this famous headline. A delighted President Harry S. Truman holds up the paper.*

Bess (left), Margaret (second from left), and President Harry Truman (right) arrive at an Inaugural Ball on January 20, 1949.

For most of Harry's second term in office, the Trumans moved back to Blair House, which Bess found more homelike and comfortable than the White House. Engineers had discovered that the Executive Mansion was collapsing and could no longer be occupied. The president's bathtub was sinking into the ceiling of the Red Room underneath, and a leg of Margaret's piano had already gone through the floor. Bess opposed replacing the

White House with a new building, as did her husband. Although she usually chose to stay in the background to preserve her privacy, she successfully helped pressure Congress for funds to gut and reconstruct the historic White House. When the work was completed in the spring of 1952, she invited the women's press corps on a personal tour of the rebuilt mansion. She proudly showed them the family's living quarters, which had been redecorated. Yet

Home Improvement

☆ ☆

Like many First Ladies, Bess decided to spruce up the White House, and especially the second-floor family quarters, to suit her tastes. She had the white woodwork washed and the rooms painted, decorated, and furnished. When Margaret's grand piano fell partway through the floor into the family dining room below, however, the Trumans realized that much more than decorating would be required. Indeed, engineers found that a past rebuilding of the attic and roof had replaced the original wood with much heavier steel and concrete. The added weight proved too heavy, and the stone walls threatened to collapse. Under the supervision of Congress and the watchful eye of President Truman, the White House was emptied out. A steel and concrete frame was erected inside the stone walls, and all the rooms were rebuilt, carefully preserving as much original detail as possible. Since most of the material cleared from the inside was not reusable, however, the government sold relic kits to recover the cost of the work. A two-dollar kit included enough pine to make a walking stick; for one hundred dollars, a kit provid-

White House repairs underway

Room renovation in progress

ed enough brick or stone to face a fireplace. By the end of the renovation in 1952, the White House included a new balcony, a full third story, and seven new rooms for a total of 132.

she still refused to give them a press conference.

Like other First Ladies, Bess worried about her husband's health under the strain of presidential responsibilities. At the conclusion of World War II, the United States and the Soviet Union had begun a "cold war," a period of mutual hostility short of war. Harry made a number of important decisions that strengthened and protected democracies all over the world. It was no wonder that he increasingly suffered from headaches and fatigue. Bess encouraged him to relax by spending weekends with him at the presidential retreat in the Maryland mountains, later named Camp David, and by having him take vacations at Key West in Florida with his poker cronies. Sometimes she joined him there. The house at 219 Delaware Street no longer gave them privacy. Once Harry became president, it became the Summer White House. A fence had to be installed to keep the curious away from their home, and Secret Service agents had to accompany them around town, much to Bess's dismay.

Presidential Hideaway

✯ ✯ ✯ ✯ ✯ ✯ ✯ ✯ ✯ ✯ ✯ ✯ ✯ ✯ ✯ ✯ ✯ ✯ ✯ ✯

Created as a safe haven for President Franklin D. Roosevelt during World War II, Camp David was first known as Shangri-La and later renamed for President Eisenhower's grandson. Located on Catoctin Mountain in Maryland, the rustic resort is a short helicopter flight from the back door of the White House. Some presidents have used Camp David more than others. By the time Richard Nixon became president, its cabins were sadly in need of repair. He saw that the camp was fixed up, and a good thing, too, as he escaped to Camp David during the heated days of the Watergate scandal. One of President Jimmy Carter's first orders was to get rid of the camp because he felt that the people didn't believe the president needed a posh vacation hideaway. After his staff convinced him to visit the camp, however, he fell in love with its woodsy, simple setting. It was a good thing that President Carter decided to keep the camp, since the greatest achievement of his presidency was the Middle East peace accord agreed on after days of talks at the secluded, peaceful Camp David.

Opposite page: President Truman strolls on a Key West beach in December 1947. Left: Bess and Harry relaxing on a Key West vacation in November 1948.

When the house in Independence became the Summer White House during Truman's presidency, a fence had to be installed to keep curious people away.

As concerned as she might be about her husband's health, Bess never anticipated that she would fear for Harry's life. Yet on November 1, 1950, at about two o'clock in the afternoon, the Trumans heard gunshots coming from the street below their window at Blair House. The couple were changing clothes before attending a ceremony at Arlington National Cemetery. Twenty-seven shots were fired in two minutes. One guard was killed and another seriously wounded. Two fanatic Puerto Rican nationalists had tried to shoot their way into Blair House to kill the president. Bess was badly shaken even though Harry commented, "Presidents have to expect such things." No longer did she try to dodge Secret Service agents or resent their intrusion in her life.

Bess was very relieved in March 1952 when Harry announced that he would not run for reelection. She could look forward to returning to Independence. To her regret, her

The scene outside Blair House after the November 1, 1950, assassination attempt

President Truman announced his decision not to run for reelection at a March 1952 Jefferson-Jackson Day dinner.

mother would not be joining her. On December 5, 1952, Madge Wallace died at the age of ninety. Bess hoped that she and Harry would be able to live simply and quietly in Independence as private citizens.

★ ★ ★ ★ ★ ★ ★ ★ ★ ★ ★ ★ ★ ★ ★

CHAPTER FIVE

Living as a Private Citizen

"Harry, the minute we get unpacked, you carry the suitcases up to the attic! That will prove we are home at last for good!" Bess ordered her husband. Crowds of well-wishers had seen them off from Washington and had greeted their arrival in Independence. Now it was time to settle in at 219 North Delaware Street as private citizens.

At first, Bess found it difficult to adjust to a life without schedules of appointments and a mother to comfort. Her bridge club met only once a week. Although she did the marketing, managed her household, listened to baseball games on the radio, and read

Crowds of well-wishers saw the Trumans off from Washington on January 20, 1953.

Another huge crowd greeted them on their arrival in Independence, Missouri.

Even though Bess played bridge once a week and an occasional game of canasta (above), did the marketing, and managed her household, she still had too much time on her hands for a while.

detective stories, there was too much time on her hands. Bess admitted to an interviewer, "Here in Independence, life is easier, slower, much more relaxed. People smile more. We have the luxury of undemanded time, but we also have the occasional dullness that goes with it."

That was quickly remedied. In the absence of presidential pensions, Harry had to earn a living, and Bess helped him with the task he chose. He decided to write his memoirs. The

Harry on his morning walk in Independence, 1953

Bess gave Harry a
large combination
seventieth birthday
party and fund-raiser
to raise money for a
library to house his
presidential papers.

Harry, Bess, and
Margaret visited
Hawaii in the spring
of 1953.

money he received for the two-volume work gave the Trumans a nest egg. The sale of the Truman family farm gave them financial security. Bess also supported his project to build a library for his presidential papers by throwing a large seventieth birthday party for him as a fund-raiser.

After the presidency, Bess and Harry began to travel. They visited Hawaii with Margaret in the spring of 1953, and then during the summer, they drove to Washington, D.C. Unfortunately, they attracted crowds along the route of their cross-country trip, and soon found themselves escorted by police motorcades, reporters, and photographers. Bess snapped, "This is the last time we go by car!" In May 1956, the Trumans toured Europe, meeting with royalty and heads of state. They returned to Europe again in 1958 with less fanfare.

On April 21, 1956, Bess and Harry attended the wedding of their daughter to Clifton Daniel at the same church where the Trumans had been married thirty-seven years earlier. Like her parents, Margaret and her new husband greeted their guests at a

The parents of the groom (left) and the bride (right) at the wedding of Margaret and Clifton Daniel

Bess, Harry, and two grandsons about to greet Margaret and Clifton as they return from a vacation

The Trumans spent Bess's seventy-sixth birthday in Bermuda with the Daniels and their two grandsons.

reception held at 219 North Delaware Street before they left on their honeymoon. Over the years, Harry and Bess were presented with four grandsons, much to their delight.

Bess quickly learned that although Harry had left office, he hadn't left politics. She was still needed to keep him in check. For example, in 1956, he persisted in backing New York Governor W. Averell Harriman as the Democratic candidate for president long after the governor's cause was hopeless. With tears in her eyes, Bess asked longtime friend Tom Evans, "Tom, can't you do something to stop Harry? He's making a fool of himself." Although her husband opposed the nomination of John F. Kennedy in 1960, he campaigned for him. To their delight, the Trumans were invited for a weekend at the White House as President and Mrs. Kennedy's guests in 1962.

They were shocked by the president's assassination a year later. As a result of that tragedy, Congress voted Secret Service protection for former presidents. Bess heartily objected to this invasion of her privacy. She refused to allow the agents to escort her husband to work. It took a phone call from President Lyndon B. Johnson to convince her to let them guard Harry at his office. She still would not let them on her property or in her home. The guards gradually gained her confidence. They did not unduly intrude on the Trumans' lives and even did little jobs around the house.

✮ ✮

While Bess Truman often expressed her distaste for the constant intrusion of the Secret Service in her life, these vigilant guardians provide an indispensable service. They are specially trained to protect the president and the first family twenty-four hours a day anywhere in the world. The service actually began, however, as a kind of detective agency for the federal government. It was officially commissioned in 1865 to combat the counterfeiting of money that had become a major problem during the Civil War. The only national law-enforcement agency at that time, it soon took on other criminal investigations. Agents worked undercover to control extortion, forgery, lottery fraud, blackmail, and terrorism. After President William McKinley was assassinated (the third president to be murdered in office) in 1901, Congress added the job of protecting the chief executive. Over the years, the role expanded to include the First Lady, the presidential family, former presidents, and other dignitaries. While security is tight at the White House, the Secret Service faces its biggest challenges when the president travels. Every move must be mapped out and every inch of the way secured in advance. In crowds, agents surround the president to form a "safe zone." It is dangerous work; Secret Service agents know they must protect the president with their own lives if necessary.

Bess and Harry had their share of poor health as they grew older. In 1954, Harry became ill while attending a performance of *Call Me Madam*, a play spoofing him and Perle Mesta, a famous Washington hostess and a friend of Bess's. His gall bladder had to be removed. Then in 1959, Bess was found to have a large noncancerous tumor. She underwent a mastectomy, the removal of a breast. She refused to let the press know what kind of operation had been performed. Bess had always been a private person, and at that time, the illnesses of public figures were not always reported to the public.

In December 1972, Harry Truman suffered his final illness. When he was hospitalized with lung problems, an exhausted Bess stayed at his bedside. On Christmas night, Margaret finally persuaded her to go home and rest. By then, Harry had slipped into unconsciousness. She was not there when he died the following morning. At Bess's insistence, the funeral was held in the auditorium of the Truman Library in Independence rather than in Washington, D.C. After the service, the American flag was removed from his casket and replaced by a blanket of red carnations, a final gift from Bess. He was buried in the library courtyard.

Bess could live in comfort for the rest of her days. Harry had left her fairly well off, and as a presidential widow, she received a pension of $20,000 a year. Margaret pleaded with her to become part of the Daniel household in New York. "I prefer to be by myself," Bess replied. She would come to visit her grandchildren, but she would not stay. In this, as in her marriage, she rejected the example set by her own mother. She was truly on her own because she had survived all her brothers as well as her husband.

On her desk, Bess placed an anniversary letter that Harry had written to her in 1957. It contained an ac-

Bess (right), Margaret and Clifton Daniel, and the Daniel children at Harry Truman's funeral on December 28, 1972

Presidents on Exhibit

✴ ✴

For many of our twentieth-century presidents, there is a library and museum somewhere in the United States. These institutions keep important presidential papers and records for scholars to use. Some even serve as presidential burial places. In addition to documents and books dealing with the serious business of the presidency, you'll also find interesting exhibits about each president's life and times. Personal belongings, photographs, and family memorabilia are arranged to tell each president's story. Things such as Herbert Hoover's fishing tackle, George Bush's baseball glove, and the collar and toys of Franklin Roosevelt's dog give visitors a glimpse into their personal lives. Visiting a presidential library and museum is a fun way to experience some American history from the presidential point of view. Perhaps there is a presidential library or museum near you:

The Franklin D. Roosevelt Library	Hyde Park, New York
The Truman Library	Independence, Missouri
The Lyndon Baines Johnson Librar	University of Texas, Austin campus
The Eisenhower Center and the Dwight D. Eisenhower Library	Abilene, Kansas
The Herbert Hoover Library	West Branch, Iowa
The John Fitzgerald Kennedy Library	Boston, Massachusetts
The Gerald R. Ford Museum	Grand Rapids, Michigan
The Jimmy Carter Presidential Library	Atlanta, Georgia
The Richard M. Nixon Library	Yorba Linda, California
The Ronald Reagan Presidential Library	Simi Valley, California
The George Bush Presidential Library	Texas A & M University, College Station

President Gerald Ford and First Lady Betty Ford (second and third from left) with Margaret Truman Daniel and Clifton Daniel at the dedication of the Harry S. Truman statue in Independence, Missouri

count of the major events of each year in their life together. It was signed, "Your no-account partner who loves you more than ever!" She often read it first thing in the morning before she did her chores. Then she visited with her friends. Occasionally, she saw Mary Paxton, her former neighbor who lived in Columbia, 120 miles (193 km) to the east.

Bess kept up her interest in politics, agreeing in 1974 to be honorary co-chair of Missouri senator Thomas Eagleton's reelection campaign. The other co-chair was St. Louis Cardinal Stan Musial, a member of baseball's Hall of Fame. "Just imagine my name linked with his," the awestruck former First Lady said. She even knew his lifetime batting average! In 1976, at the age of ninety-one, Bess served as Congressman Jim Symington's honorary campaign chair in his unsuccessful run for the Senate. She also greeted President and Mrs. Gerald Ford at her home on North Delaware Street. They were visiting Independence to dedicate a statue of Harry in the town square, but Bess was too frail to attend.

Until she became weakened with arthritis, a crippling joint disease, Bess refused to have live-in help. Finally, nurses moved in with her. One of them read her Margaret's first novel, *Murder at the White House*. By then, Bess's eyesight had failed. "Good job," she told her daughter. As a fan of detective stories, she was delighted that Margaret had become a mystery novelist.

In 1981, Bess suffered a stroke, a blood clot in the brain, that left her unable to communicate. She died on

---

Margaret Truman (b. 1924)

✫ ✫

Unlike her mother, who was a very private person, Margaret Truman pursued a public career. She performed with the Detroit Symphony Orchestra on a nationwide radio broadcast at the age of twenty-three and sang before a live audience of 20,000 people at the Hollywood Bowl the same year. Her first television appearance came on Ed Sullivan's *Toast of the Town* show in 1950. When her parents left the White House, she moved to New York to continue her work with the National Broadcasting Company (NBC). In New York, she met Clifton Daniel, the foreign news editor of *The New York Times*. They were married and had four children. Today, Margaret is a well-known author. Her works include biographies of both of her parents and a series of murder mysteries set at famous Washington, D.C., sites such as the White House, the Supreme Court, and the Pentagon.

Margaret during a radio broadcast

October 18, 1982, at the age of nine-ty-seven.

Three First Ladies—Nancy Reagan, Betty Ford, and Rosalynn Carter—attended the simple funeral service for Bess in the little church where she and Harry had been married. She was buried beside her husband, covered by a blanket of roses, her favorite flower. Bess Truman had lived longer than any other First Lady. She never put on airs and she never forgot who she was, a dignified, private, small-town woman who happened to have been the wife of the thirty-third president of the United States.

Bess Truman's coffin was covered with a blanket of roses, her favorite flower.

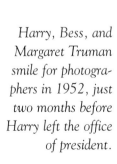

Harry, Bess, and Margaret Truman smile for photographers in 1952, just two months before Harry left the office of president.

Portrait of America, 1982: Preppies and Punks

☆ ☆

When she died at the age of ninety-seven, Bess Truman had lived through nineteen presidencies, including her husband's. In 1982, Ronald Reagan and his Republican administration set a conservative national mood. First Lady Nancy Reagan inspired a return to elegance and formality. A spreading preoccupation with wealth and status led the fashion conscious to "dress for success." Working women adopted the masculine blue "power" suit as their uniform, hoping to toughen their image in the workplace. "Preppies" cultivated a rich but casual look that made loafers, pink polo shirts, and khaki pants the rage. The aerobics and fitness craze elevated sneakers to high fashion. On television, Americans eagerly followed the sagas of wealthy families on the evening soaps *Dallas* and *Dynasty*.

Pop culture bit back. Break dancing took the city streets by storm. Michael Jackson and Madonna popularized a brassy urban glamour imitated by young people everywhere. Punk rockers pierced their ears and spiked their hair. Unbelievably, more American homes had television sets than indoor plumbing.

Americans also shared a deepening recession in 1982. This slowing of the economy dealt the working class a difficult double blow: jobs grew scarce and the cost of living rose. Eleven million Americans were out of work, creating the highest rate of unemployment since the Great Depression of the 1930s. The poverty level stood at its highest since 1967, with 14 percent of Americans living on less than $10,000 a year. Despite the expanding African-American middle class, the poverty rate among blacks climbed to 34 percent.

Two monuments in the nation's capital figured in the news that year. The long-awaited Vietnam Veterans Memorial was unveiled, its shimmering black stone surface bearing the name of every soldier killed during that war. Not far away, the Washington Monument came under unsuccessful threat by a protester against nuclear weapons. That tall white spire had been dedicated the year of Bess's birth and by 1982 had become one of the nation's best-beloved national symbols.

The Presidents and Their First Ladies

President	Birth–Death	First Lady	Birth–Death
1789–1797			
George Washington	1732–1799	Martha Dandridge Custis Washington	1731–1802
1797–1801			
John Adams	1735–1826	Abigail Smith Adams	1744–1818
1801–1809			
Thomas Jefferson†	1743–1826		
1809–1817			
James Madison	1751–1836	Dolley Payne Todd Madison	1768–1849
1817–1825			
James Monroe	1758–1831	Elizabeth Kortright Monroe	1768–1830
1825–1829			
John Quincy Adams	1767–1848	Louisa Catherine Johnson Adams	1775–1852
1829–1837			
Andrew Jackson†	1767–1845		
1837–1841			
Martin Van Buren†	1782–1862		
1841			
William Henry Harrison‡	1773–1841		
1841–1845			
John Tyler	1790–1862	Letitia Christian Tyler (1841–1842)	1790–1842
		Julia Gardiner Tyler (1844–1845)	1820–1889
1845–1849			
James K. Polk	1795–1849	Sarah Childress Polk	1803–1891
1849–1850			
Zachary Taylor	1784–1850	Margaret Mackall Smith Taylor	1788–1852
1850–1853			
Millard Fillmore	1800–1874	Abigail Powers Fillmore	1798–1853
1853–1857			
Franklin Pierce	1804–1869	Jane Means Appleton Pierce	1806–1863
1857–1861			
James Buchanan*	1791–1868		
1861–1865			
Abraham Lincoln	1809–1865	Mary Todd Lincoln	1818–1882
1865–1869			
Andrew Johnson	1808–1875	Eliza McCardle Johnson	1810–1876
1869–1877			
Ulysses S. Grant	1822–1885	Julia Dent Grant	1826–1902
1877–1881			
Rutherford B. Hayes	1822–1893	Lucy Ware Webb Hayes	1831–1889
1881			
James A. Garfield	1831–1881	Lucretia Rudolph Garfield	1832–1918
1881–1885			
Chester A. Arthur†	1829–1886		

† wife died before he took office   ‡ wife too ill to accompany him to Washington   * never married

1885–1889			
Grover Cleveland	1837–1908	Frances Folsom Cleveland	1864–1947
1889–1893			
Benjamin Harrison	1833–1901	Caroline Lavinia Scott Harrison	1832–1892
1893–1897			
Grover Cleveland	1837–1908	Frances Folsom Cleveland	1864–1947
1897–1901			
William McKinley	1843–1901	Ida Saxton McKinley	1847–1907
1901–1909			
Theodore Roosevelt	1858–1919	Edith Kermit Carow Roosevelt	1861–1948
1909–1913			
William Howard Taft	1857–1930	Helen Herron Taft	1861–1943
1913–1921			
Woodrow Wilson	1856–1924	Ellen Louise Axson Wilson (1913–1914)	1860–1914
		Edith Bolling Galt Wilson (1915–1921)	1872–1961
1921–1923			
Warren G. Harding	1865–1923	Florence Kling Harding	1860–1924
1923–1929			
Calvin Coolidge	1872–1933	Grace Anna Goodhue Coolidge	1879–1957
1929–1933			
Herbert Hoover	1874–1964	Lou Henry Hoover	1874–1944
1933–1945			
Franklin D. Roosevelt	1882–1945	Anna Eleanor Roosevelt	1884–1962
1945–1953			
Harry S. Truman	1884–1972	Bess Wallace Truman	1885–1982
1953–1961			
Dwight D. Eisenhower	1890–1969	Mamie Geneva Doud Eisenhower	1896–1979
1961–1963			
John F. Kennedy	1917–1963	Jacqueline Bouvier Kennedy	1929–1994
1963–1969			
Lyndon B. Johnson	1908–1973	Claudia Taylor (Lady Bird) Johnson	1912–
1969–1974			
Richard Nixon	1913–1994	Patricia Ryan Nixon	1912–1993
1974–1977			
Gerald Ford	1913–	Elizabeth Bloomer Ford	1918–
1977–1981			
James Carter	1924–	Rosalynn Smith Carter	1927–
1981–1989			
Ronald Reagan	1911–	Nancy Davis Reagan	1923–
1989–1993			
George Bush	1924–	Barbara Pierce Bush	1925–
1993–			
William Jefferson Clinton	1946–	Hillary Rodham Clinton	1947–

Bess Wallace Truman Timeline

1885	★	Bess Wallace is born on February 13
		Washington Monument is dedicated
1886	★	Statue of Liberty is dedicated
1888	★	Benjamin Harrison is elected president
1889	★	Flood in Johnstown, Pennsylvania, kills 2,295 people
1892	★	Ellis Island immigration center opens
		Grover Cleveland is elected president
1893	★	Economic depression hits the United States
1896	★	William McKinley is elected president
		First moving pictures are shown in New York City
		First Ford automobile is built in Detroit
1898	★	Spanish-American War is fought, resulting in the United States annexing Puerto Rico, Guam, and the Philippines
		United States annexes Hawaii
		William McKinley is reelected president
1901	★	President McKinley is assassinated
		Theodore Roosevelt becomes president
1903	★	Wright brothers fly their airplane for the first time
1904	★	Theodore Roosevelt is elected president
1906	★	Theodore Roosevelt receives the Nobel Peace Prize
1908	★	William Howard Taft is elected president
1909	★	National Association for the Advancement of Colored People (NAACP) is founded
1912	★	Woodrow Wilson is elected president
		Titanic sinks in the North Atlantic

1914 ★ Panama Canal is completed
World War I begins

1915 ★ *Lusitania* is sunk by a German submarine

1916 ★ Woodrow Wilson is reelected president

1917 ★ United States enters World War I
Harry S. Truman enlists in the Missouri National Guard

1918 ★ United States and its allies win World War I

1919 ★ Bess Wallace marries Harry S. Truman

1920 ★ Warren G. Harding is elected president
Woodrow Wilson receives the Nobel Peace Prize

1922 ★ Lincoln Memorial is dedicated

1923 ★ President Harding dies
Calvin Coolidge becomes president

1924 ★ Mary Margaret Truman is born
Calvin Coolidge is elected president

1927 ★ Charles Lindbergh flies solo across the Atlantic Ocean

1928 ★ Herbert Hoover is elected president

1929 ★ Stock market crashes, which starts the Great Depression

1932 ★ Amelia Earhart becomes the first woman to fly solo across the Atlantic Ocean
Franklin D. Roosevelt is elected president

1933 ★ President Roosevelt begins the New Deal

1934 ★ Harry S. Truman is elected to the U.S. Senate

1935 ★ Congress passes the Social Security Act

1936 ★ Franklin D. Roosevelt is reelected president

1939 ★ World War II begins

1940 ★ Franklin D. Roosevelt is reelected president
Harry S. Truman is reelected to the U.S. Senate

1941	★	Japanese bomb Pearl Harbor United States enters World War II
1944	★	Franklin D. Roosevelt is reelected president Harry S. Truman is elected vice president
1945	★	President Roosevelt dies Harry S. Truman becomes president Germany surrenders to the Allies in Europe United States drops atomic bombs on Japan Japan surrenders, ending World War II
1947	★	Jackie Robinson becomes the first African-American to play major-league baseball
1948	★	Marshall Plan extends aid to war-torn Europe Berlin Airlift begins Harry S. Truman is elected president
1949	★	United Nations Headquarters is dedicated in New York City
1950	★	President Truman sends U.S. forces to fight in Korean War
1952	★	Dwight D. Eisenhower is elected president
1953	★	Korean War ends
1954	★	Supreme Court declares segregated schools to be unconstitutional
1956	★	Dwight D. Eisenhower is reelected president
1960	★	John F. Kennedy is elected president
1961	★	First Americans fly in space United States sends aid and advisers to South Vietnam
1963	★	John F. Kennedy is assassinated Lyndon B. Johnson becomes president
1964	★	Civil Rights Act is signed Lyndon B. Johnson is elected president
1965	★	Malcolm X is assassinated U.S. sends troops to Vietnam

1966	★	Medicare Act is signed
		United States has 400,000 troops in Vietnam
1967	★	Antiwar protest is held at the Pentagon
1968	★	Civil Rights Act is signed
		Martin Luther King Jr. and Robert F. Kennedy are assassinated
		Richard M. Nixon is elected president
1969	★	President Nixon begins withdrawing U.S. soldiers from Vietnam
1970	★	Antiwar protests rock college campuses
1972	★	Last U.S. ground troops are withdrawn from Vietnam
		Burglary at the Watergate Complex is reported
		Richard Nixon is reelected president
		Harry S. Truman dies
1973	★	Vice President Spiro Agnew resigns
		Gerald Ford becomes vice president
1974	★	Richard M. Nixon resigns from office
		Gerald Ford becomes president
1975	★	South Vietnam falls to the Communists
1976	★	Jimmy Carter is elected president
		United States celebrates its bicentennial
1977	★	President Carter issues a pardon to Vietnam War draft evaders
1978	★	People's Republic of China and the United States begin full diplomatic ties
1979	★	Iranians seize U.S. Embassy in Tehran and hold American hostages
1980	★	Ronald Reagan is elected president
1981	★	Iranians release the U.S. hostages
		Sandra Day O'Connor becomes the first woman appointed to the U.S. Supreme Court
1982	★	Bess Wallace Truman dies on October 18

Fast Facts about
Bess Wallace Truman

Born: February 13, 1885, in Independence, Missouri

Died: October 18, 1982, in Independence, Missouri

Burial Site: The Truman Library Courtyard, Independence, Missouri

Parents: David Willock Wallace and Margaret "Madge" Gates Wallace

Education: Elementary school and high school in Independence; Barstow Finishing School in Kansas City, Missouri

Marriage: To Harry S. Truman on June 28, 1919, until his death in 1972

Children: Mary Margaret

Places She Lived: Independence, Missouri (1885–1903, 1905–1919, 1922–1982); Colorado Springs, Colorado (1903–1905); Kansas City, Missouri (1919–1922); Washington, D.C. (1935–1953)

Major Achievements:

⭑ Did the bookkeeping for White House expenses, and carefully supervised all money spent at the White House while First Lady.

⭑ Acted as a personal adviser during her husband's campaigns and terms in office.

⭑ Helped her husband write his speeches throughout his political career.

⭑ Started a Spanish class at the White House to improve Pan-American relations.

⭑ Pressured Congress for funds to repair the crumbling structure of the White House.

⭑ Helped her husband write his memoirs after he left the presidency.

⭑ Supported her husband's project of building a library for his presidential papers by hosting a fund-raising party.

⭑ Served as honorary chair for U.S. senator Thomas Eagleton's reelection campaign (1974) and for Congressman Jim Symington's campaign for the U.S. Senate (1976).

Fast Facts about
Harry S. Truman's Presidency

Terms of Office: Became the thirty-third president of the United States upon the death of Franklin Delano Roosevelt on April 12, 1945; elected president in his own right in 1948 and served until January 20, 1953

Vice President: No vice president from April 12, 1945, to January 20, 1949; Alben William Barkley (1949–1953)

Major Policy Decisions and Legislation:

* Gave the order to drop atomic bombs on Hiroshima (August 6, 1945) and Nagaski (August 9, 1945) in Japan.
* Signed the Marshall Plan into law (April 3, 1948), extending aid to war-torn countries in Europe.
* Ordered the Berlin Airlift (June 26, 1948), after the USSR blockaded West Berlin.
* Signed the North Atlantic Treaty (July 25, 1949), making the United States a member of NATO.
* Ordered U.S. air and naval forces to aid the South Korean government (June 27, 1950), bringing the United States into the Korean War.
* Signed the peace treaty with Japan (April 15, 1952), officially ending World War II.

Major Events:

* Germany surrenders to the Allied forces (May 7, 1945), ending World War II in Europe.
* Japan surrenders to the Allies (August 14, 1945), ending World War II.
* President Truman appointed Frederick Moore Vinson as chief justice of the U.S. Supreme Court (June 21, 1946) and three associate justices to the U.S. Supreme Court: Harold Hitz Burton (October 1, 1945), Thomas Campbell Clark (August 24, 1949), and Sherman Minton (October 12, 1949).
* Puerto Rican nationalists tried to assassinate President Truman in Blair House (November 1, 1950). Puerto Rico became a U.S. commonwealth (July 25, 1952).

Where to Visit

The Capitol Building
Constitution Avenue
Washington, D.C. 20510
(202) 225-3121

Harry S. Truman Library & Museum
U.S. Highway 24 & Delaware
Independence, Missouri 64050-1798
(800) 833-1225
e-mail: library@truman.nara.gov

Museum of American History of the
    Smithsonian Institution
"First Ladies: Political and Public Image"
14th Street and Constitution Avenue NW
Washington, D.C.
(202) 357-2008

National Archives
Constitution Avenue
Washington, D.C.
(202) 501-5000

The National First Ladies Library
The Saxton McKinley House
331 South Market Avenue
Canton, Ohio 44702

White House
1600 Pennsylvania Avenue
Washington, D.C. 20500
Visitor's Office: (202) 456-7041

White House Historical Association
740 Jackson Place NW
Washington, D.C. 20503
(202) 737-8292

Online Sites of Interest

The First Ladies of the United States of America
http://www2.whitehouse.gov/WH/glimpse/firstladies/html/firstladies.html
A portrait and biographical sketch of each First Lady plus links to other White House sites

Harry S. Truman Library & Museum
http://www.lbjlib.utexas.edu/truman/
Includes a description of the exhibits in the museum; programs and events; a guide to historical materials at the library; points of interest in Kansas City and Independence; and a list of places to eat in the area plus links to other sites

History Happens
http://www.usahistory.com/presidents
A site that contains fast facts about Harry S. Truman

Internet Public Library, Presidents of the United States (IPL POTUS)
http://www.ipl.org/ref/POTUS/hstruman.html
An excellent site with much information about Harry Truman, including personal information and facts about his presidency; many links to other sites including biographies and other Internet resources

The National First Ladies Library
http://www.firstladies.org
The first virtual library devoted to the lives and legacies of America's First Ladies; includes a bibliography of books, articles, letters, and manuscripts by and about the nation's First Ladies; also includes a virtual tour, with pictures, of the restored Saxton McKinley House in Canton, Ohio, which houses the library

The White House
http://www.whitehouse.gov/WH/Welcome.html
Information about the current president and vice president; White House history and tours; biographies of past presidents and their families; a virtual tour of the historic building, current events, and much more

The White House for Kids
http://www.whitehouse.gov/WH/kids/html/kidshome.html
Socks the cat is your guide to this site, which includes information about White House kids, past and present; famous "First Pets," past and present; historic moments of the presidency; several issues of a newsletter called "Inside the White House," and more

For Further Reading

Dolan, Edward F. *America in World War I*. Brookfield, Conn.: Millbrook Press, 1996.

Farley, Karin C. *Harry Truman: The Man from Independence*. Englewood Cliffs, N.J.: Julian Messner, 1989.

Ferrell, Robert H. (ed.). *Dear Bess: The Letters from Harry to Bess Truman, 1910–1959*. New York: W. W. Norton & Company, 1983.

Gormley, Beatrice. *First Ladies*. New York: Scholastic, Inc., 1997.

Gould, Lewis L. (ed.). *American First Ladies: Their Lives and Their Legacy*. New York: Garland Publishing, 1996.

Jacobson, Doranne. *Presidents and First Ladies of the United States*. New York: Smithmark Publishers, Inc., 1995.

Klapthor, Margaret Brown. *The First Ladies*. Washington, D.C.: White House Historical Association, 1994.

Kummer, Patricia K. *Missouri*. One Nation series. Mankato, Minn.: Capstone Press, 1998.

Mayo, Edith P. (ed.). *The Smithsonian Book of the First Ladies: Their Lives, Times, and Issues*. New York: Henry Holt, 1996.

O'Neal, Michael. *President Truman and the Atomic Bomb*. San Diego: Greenhaven Press, Inc., 1990.

Sandak, Cass. *The Trumans*. New York: Crestwood House, 1992.

Stein, R. Conrad. *The Great Depression*. Cornerstones of Freedom series. Chicago: Childrens Press, 1993.

Stewart, Gail B. *World War I*. America's Wars series. San Diego: Lucent Books, 1991.

Sullivan, George. *The Day the Women Got the Vote: A Photo History of the Women's Rights Movement*. New York: Scholastic Inc., 1994.

Index

Page numbers in **boldface type** indicate illustrations

108

Photo Identifications

Cover: Official White House portrait of Bess Wallace Truman by Martha Greta Kempton
Page 8: Bess as a young girl
Page 20: Bess as a young woman before her marriage; Harry carried this picture in his wallet during World War I.
Page 34: Bess with baby Margaret, 1924
Page 54: Official White House portraits of President Harry S. Truman and First Lady Bess Wallace Truman by Martha Greta Kempton
Page 82: Bess and Harry Truman on the porch of their Independence home after Harry left the office of president

Photo Credits©

White House Historical Association— Cover, 54 (both pictures), 98 (bottom), 100, 101 (bottom)
The Harry S. Truman Library— 8, 11 (middle and bottom), 12, 13, 15, 16 (both pictures), 17 (both pictures), 18 (both pictures), 20, 22, 23, 26 (left), 34, 36 (bottom), 39 (both pictures), 40 (both pictures), 42, 45, 62, (bottom left), 74 (bottom), 98 (top), 99 (middle); Bradley Smith, photographer, 82, 85 (top); *The New York Times,* 87 (bottom); UPI News Photograph, 94 (bottom)
Jackson County Historical Society— 11 (top)
AP/Wide World Photos— 14 (both pictures), 19, 23 (right), 41 (right), 43 (right), 44 (top), 47, 53 (bottom), 56 (bottom), 62 (top and bottom right), 69 (bottom), 72, 75 (top), 80, 85 (bottom), 87 (top), 99 (bottom)
Kansas City Museum, Kansas City, Missouri— 24
Stock Montage, Inc.— 25, 32, 49, 50, 51 (top), 56 (top), 57 (right), 58 (top), 59, 60 (top), 64, 66 (both pictures), 68 (bottom), 74 (top), 75 (bottom), 76, 81 (top), 93, 99 (top)
UPI/Corbis-Bettmann— 27, 29 (right), 30, 31, 33, 36 (top), 37, 44 (bottom), 46, 51 (bottom), 52 (both pictures), 53 (top), 57 (left), 58 (bottom), 60 (bottom), 61, 67 (all three pictures), 68 (top), 69 (top), 71, 73, 77 (both pictures), 78, 79, 81 (bottom), 84 (both pictures), 86 (both pictures), 88, 89, 92, 94 (top)
Corbis-Bettmann— 29 (left), 43 (left)
Kansas City Chamber of Commerce/courtesy Harry S. Truman Library— 41 (left)
Reproduced by permission of the Richard Nixon Library, Yorba Linda, California— 101 (top)

About the Author

Barbara Silberdick Feinberg graduated with honors from Wellesley College where she was elected to Phi Beta Kappa. She holds a Ph.D. in political science from Yale University. Among her more recent books are *Watergate : Scandal in the White House*, *American Political Scandals Past and Present*, *The National Government*, *State Governments*, *Local Governments*, *Words in the News: A Student's Dictionary of American Government and Politics*, *Harry S. Truman*, *John Marshall: The Great Chief Justice*, *Electing the President*, *The Cabinet*, *Hiroshima and Nagasaki*, *Black Tuesday: The Stock Market Crash of 1929*, *Term Limits for Congress*, *The Constitutional Amendments*, and *Next in Line: The American Vice Presidency*. She has also written *Marx and Marxism*, *The Constitution: Yesterday, Today, and Tomorrow*, and *Franklin D. Roosevelt: Gallant President*. She is a contributor to *The Young Reader's Companion to American History*.

Mrs. Feinberg lives in New York City with her younger son Douglas and two Yorkshire terriers, Katie and Holly. Among her hobbies are growing African violets, collecting antique autographs of historical personalities, listening to the popular music of the 1920s and 1930s, and working out in exercise classes.